POET TREE

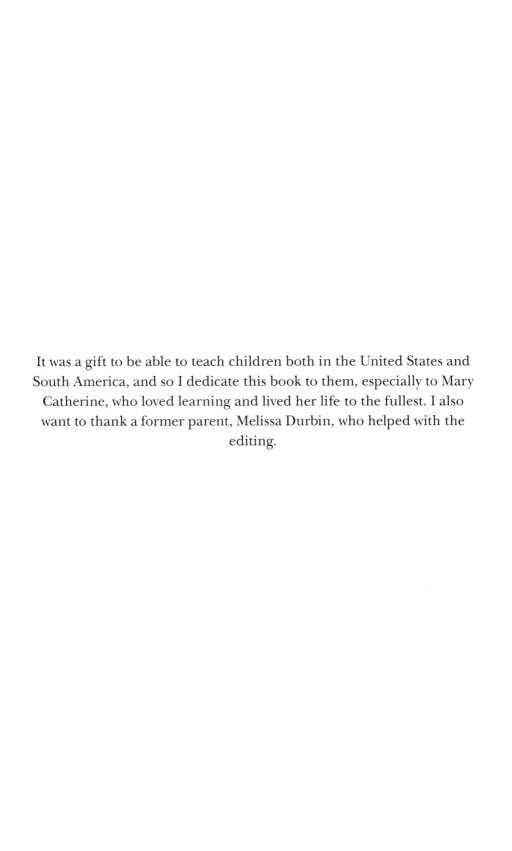

It was a gift to be able to teach children both in the United States and South America, and so I dedicate this book to them, especially to Mary Catherine, who loved learning and lived her life to the fullest. I also want to thank a former parent, Melissa Durbin, who helped with the editing.

MARY CATHERINE

A bundle of smiles, sparkling eyes:
So encouraging until you realize
She contributed and helped in every single way
Wise beyond her years, I certainly would say.

Our first literature book, *The Family Tree,*
The best book she had ever read, naturally.
She knew how to show she truly cared,
Always animated and willing to share.

A light vanished in the night sky
When Mary Catherine said good-bye.

Learning about her ancestors
During the immigration study.
Presenting on the special day
During the Huddled Masses Café.

Characteristically optimistic,
She loved art, history, and music
And was always willing to go the extra mile
With her broad smile and own special style.

A light dimmed in the night sky
When Mary Catherine said good-bye.

A positive influence on those she had touched,
She was appreciated so very much,
For both her talent and fun-loving personality,
Which helped make our positive community a reality.

A light extinguished on the day that
Mary Catherine went away.

CONTENTS

Chapter 1 Why Write Poetry?. 1

Chapter 2 Beginning-of-the-Year Activities. 5

Chapter 3 Exploring Our Five Senses 24

Chapter 4 Trees, Trees, and More Trees 38

Chapter 5 The World and Us. 50

Chapter 6 All Kinds of Animals. 64

Chapter 7 Color Poems. 85

Chapter 8 Dreams, Magical Creatures, Special Places,
           and People. 95

Chapter 9 Learning Parts of Speech through Poetry. 106

Chapter 10 Learning from Established Poets. 111

Chapter 11 Writing Poetry Across the Curriculum 134

Chapter 12 Mentored by the Masters 149

Chapter 13 Conclusion. 165

Chapter 1

WHY WRITE POETRY?

You may ask, "Why write poetry?" I know that when I introduce children to rich, lively verse, I am introducing them to vivid, skillfully crafted language. Everything a person needs to know about reading and writing exists within poetry. To appreciate a poem, a person has to understand language. When children learn how to write poetry, they are invited to understand and to view themselves and the world in new ways. Their lives are enriched as they discover creatively used sounds and rhythms. In the process, they learn to use tools. One tool they may learn to use is the thesaurus to find the right word for a line of poetry. Another is the dictionary or a book of rhyming words. Each student should have a spiral notebook dedicated to poetry. All of their exercises and observations should be recorded in it. Finally, it enables them to appreciate imagery and figurative language. Also, if students are studying poetry through other units such as African American history, they are given a chance to learn about another culture.

Each year we had a major poetry unit, which was integrated into every aspect of our learning during the year. I think you will be quite impressed by how freely the children share their ideas, experiences, and insights. During our immigration unit one year, I had the children get into family groups where they wrote a collaborative poem expressing why they had left their country for America, wrote a short description or biography, and included a recipe of the food that they were bringing from "their country" to the Huddled Masses Café. At the café, where all the parents attended, we had several adult immigrants who shared their experiences with the children.

We also had a poetry tea every year, usually held in early May because our Great Brain Project, another major event, was in June. The very first tea was in the early 1990s and was held in the classroom. Years later, when Danny was going to present his poetry, he found a note in his pocket written by Rachel, his babysitter and one of my former students, which said, "Enjoy the poetry tea. It was my favorite activity because I was able to read my poem to my dad." Later, the teas grew larger and became more like English teas, with desserts and sandwiches, and parents and other important guests attended and heard the children sharing at least one poem of their choosing. Some years, children had friends provide instrumental accompaniment; other years we prepared choral readings as well as the individual poems. The subjects were as varied as the children themselves. The tea became a favorite activity. When there was school construction in our resource center, we could not use the usual space. One of my former families volunteered to host the tea in their home. After the tea, each child received an anthology of all of the class poems. This served as a way of preserving a memory and reaching a larger audience. Selecting poems for this book was a challenging decision because there were just so many well-written poems, but I was on a limited budget. People other than educators will enjoy them and at the same time be astounded by what nine- and ten-year-olds were capable of writing. The poems in this book may also be models for children in other teachers' classrooms. Poetry is directly linked to reading comprehension and vocabulary. As they read, children try to figure out what the authors meant by writing their particular poems during a time period. Children also learn about what was happening in the world at that time.

When selecting the right word for what they had in mind, children learned about figurative language (personification, metaphors, similes, to name a few). This is especially important when writing a brief poem. Children also became keen observers, just as they had to be in science and other core subject areas. Poetry stimulates the imagination and encourages writers to see the world through a different lens. To be able to write the way you want to write, you will need to listen to poets as they read their writing. Just as in any sport or art, there are separate subskills that need to be practiced over and over again in order to learn them. Given a variety of formats, some may find the seventeen-syllable structure or format of haikus easier, but to write a seventeen-syllable poem means that the author uses precise and vivid language and has selected a specific topic in mind. Haikus are a Japanese form of poetry which is usually three lines long with a total of seventeen syllables and is about some aspect of nature or human emotions. Writers truly begin to look at the world in a new way.

Young writers have to learn the structure of poetry as well as basic English and punctuation. I began with writing poetry during first few weeks of school when, as a class, we were already developing a learning community. The poetry activities served as an important get-to-know-you activity for September. I named this book *Poet Tree* partly because for many years I used the tree as a metaphor in the classroom. The forest is one of the biomes of our area, and the other one is the prairie. The term also refers to family trees; like families, the tree's roots are embedded in the ground with its trunk supporting it, and the branches are the children—the fruit or outgrowth from the trunk.

Writing poetry can be a journey through the senses. Using the senses of taste, smell, touch, sight, hearing, and feeling/emotion allows children to play with and experience the joy of language as they express their feelings and experiences. During our poetry unit, we studied figurative language and imagery, different kinds of poetry, and published poets. Exposure to different poets is like studying artists who painted in different styles and subject matter partly because of the time in which they lived. The children wrote about nature, animals, families, trees, seasons, memories, songs, hopes and dreams, secret places, and feelings/emotions, and they wrote poems in the style of different poets.

Chapter 2

BEGINNING-OF-THE-YEAR ACTIVITIES

Ｍy children became a community of writers early on when they shared their ideas, worked on collaborative writing projects, and helped each other with the revising process. *Poet Tree* is a collection of poetry primarily written during the first two-thirds of the year. Children wrote about the world, emotions, animals, and hopes and dreams, as well as specific authors. It represents about twenty years of teaching because teachers improve year after year as they try new ideas and refine what they have done in the past. In the beginning-of-the-year, we wrote poems to share about ourselves. Open-ended patterns are needed. Here is the one I used:

Pattern: Child's Name Song
                         With many…
                       My song moves…
                     And dances like…
                       My song is a…
             In the dark, in the dark moonlight.
                         With many…

My song moves like…
And dances…
My song is a…

The children used figurative language before they actually knew what it was. The first activity was putting the poems on leaves and placing them on the large tree located on the bulletin board in the hallway. Here are two poems:

JOE'S SONG

My song sounds like people whispering in the wintery forest.
It looks and feels like a bright light reflecting off of a mirror.
My song dreams of army battles.
My song moves like a cheetah chasing its prey.
My song dances like a cricket in a flower garden.
My song is as loud as a lion roaring across his kingdom.
By Joe H. (fourth grader)

ISABELLA'S SONG

My song is like stars moving in and out of the dark moonlight
Shining in the sky. It feels loud with the stars whispering and
As quiet as a bird chirping in the dark, in the dark moonlight.
The stars move slowly while dancing in the night like a fairy
Who flies from one sleeping person to another.
I dream of a star that will shoot into my hands, like a shooting star.
By Isabella R. (fourth grader)

The second activity was making a "Metaphor Map of Me." My fourth graders were asked to create an object that represented their brain, their heart, their hands, and their feet. They could come up with other comparisons, but the four sections needed to be completed because of what they represented. When they were done, they would display pictures of the objects in the approximate place on the map/paper that would represent their bodies. *The brain is how you think.* Questions are key. Some choices included a toaster, a popcorn popper, or a puzzle. Of course, there are many, many more, but these are obvious and easy to understand. When white bread is put in the toaster, it gently turns brown, and when it is ready, it pops up. A popcorn popper has kernels going everywhere within the machine. That person who can brainstorm and think of lots of ideas is creative. The brain also represents creativity.

Children need to think of their hearts. What do they love, and what can they not live without? That representation is the center of a child's world. Their outstretched arms are what they are working toward. What are their goals? The feet represent where they are planted or rooted. What do they want to do when they grow up? Besides having a brainstorming session, teachers need to make the contents into a planner or planning sheet. Modeling is key for success. These two activities gave everyone an idea of the classroom community and provided the foundation for that community. I shared a poem of what I had hoped our community would become that year.

PARAGRAPH WRITING: PLANNING "THE METAPHOR OF ME" ACTIVITY

The writing assignment is a paragraph explaining the map that you made of yourself. You will need to list the main ideas below. Also, you will need to think of a catchy topic sentence that introduces the idea. For example, I might talk about being like a tapestry in my topic sentence, and then my other supporting points would relate in some way to the tapestry. Some people prefer to write the topic sentence first, while others like to do it last. Just make sure you discuss your points in a logical order.

List:

Brain: _____

Feet: _____

Heart:_____

Hands _____

Activities: _____

Here are two biographical poems that serve as a way of the children's getting to know each other. The title is the first name. Line 1: three descriptive words about the person. Line 2: family relationships. Line 3: three things that the person loves. Line 4: three or four ways that the person feels. Line 5: what scares him or her. Line 6: who would the person like to meet. Line 7: what the person is afraid of. Line 8: where the person would like to visit. Line 8: where the person lives. Line 9: the person's last name.

RAY

Athletic, video watcher, and electronic game player
Sibling of Sam and Anna,
Son of Robert and Leigh
Lover of dogs, video games, and basketball
Who feels nervous, happy and sad
Who fears robbers, hurricanes, and dying
Who would like to see Tracy McGrady and Miami
Resident of Winnetka, Sunset Road
By Ray W. (fourth grader)

STEPHANY

Funny, friendly, creative, and tall
Sibling of Lexy, daughter of Marilyn and Chad
Lover of my sister, art, and food
Who feels hungry, jumpy and energetic,
Who fears earthquakes, tornados, and canyons
Who would like to see the inside of the Louvre,
The volcanoes of Hawaii, and the hot springs in
Santorin, Greece
Resident of Winnetka, Sheridan Road
By Stephany P. (fourth grader)

The beginning-of-the-year is an important time to create a theme that can be used throughout the year. When I was in England, I bought and took pictures of as many gardens as possible. I had seen what had been done in different schools in Britain to foster using a theme and all of the activities that spiraled out from that theme. I had seen what a school had created when water had been their focus. You can imagine the science, social studies, reading, and writing that would stem from this study. Reflection is one the main parts of a water study. When I taught a fourth- and fifth-grade multi-age, we focused on Peter Rabbit. The older children created big books that would help their first-grade buddies develop their reading. As a celebration, we had a "Peter Rabbit" tea for the children, their parents, and special guests. As a teacher, you should brainstorm all the ways that your topic may be used within your classroom. Put the topic in the middle of a blank piece of paper. The topic serves as a hub, and the related ideas are like the spokes of a wheel or branches of a tree. From our Peter Rabbit study, the first-grade teacher developed a farm unit, an outgrowth of our study, which was used by the other first-grade teachers.

It is important for the children to be surrounded by excellent literature. I would select a poem per week that the children would read over and over again. Some would memorize the poem. We would discuss the poem during the week. In the weekly newsletter, I would include a copy of the poem and talk about why the poem was chosen.

The following two paragraphs are the ones I included with the poem "Native Trees," by W. S. Merton:

> Children and parents do not always see the same thing the same way, and this poem speaks to that. Parents may think of trees primarily as furniture, frame for housing, and other utilitarian things. Children may wonder more about trees themselves, the shade they give, and other matters unconcerned with the uses to which they may be put.

Rhyming and humor are two devices often used to entice children into the world of poetry. This poem contains neither of those elements, yet it has appeared in a collection of children's poetry because it captures the divide between adulthood and childhood.

You may say, "How can I find the time to find all of the poems?" Take baby steps at first. Provide the poems on a bimonthly or monthly schedule. Use a parent resource to help you. Parents can be invaluable and often want to help.

Usually in the beginning of the year, the Open House is a time for parents to visit the classroom and see where their children spend their time. Introduce your students to different songs. The song lyrics are like poems, and children readily learn the words. Once I chose the song "These are a Few of my Favorite Things," from "A Sound of Music.". The class was divided into small groups of four to six students and were asked to create their own lyrics. After revising and practicing their songs, the children were videotaped so that their songs could be shared at Open House.

Another kind of poem we did in the beginning of the year was a list poem. Children think about where they collect or stash their belongings and what those things say about themselves. If a child has five books, pictures of a certain place, and a calendar, then one could surmise that the person enjoys reading, wants to travel or visit a certain place, and has friends. The first two examples are ones written about the space under the bed and the desk at school. The school desk is a place that many children consider their "special place" filled with colorful note pads and pencils, pictures of friends, and other significant items. List poems are fun and give the students a chance to be silly and write like e.e. cummings, a poet who doesn't follow the usual rules. Giving them an example shows the children that the assignment isn't difficult and reveals something about themselves.

UNDER MY BED

What is under my bed?
Well let's find out!
There is a lot fun! There are spinning tops that the top pops off
and spins.
There is a clinking monkey that's hair is pink and spiky.
Hey look! It's a little black and white penguin that
Might not put up a fight.
That reminds me of New York. It's a toy of the Statue of Liberty
that kind of looks like a boy. And there's a teeny, tiny globe that
feels pretty spiky.
Look there's something in the back; I don't think it is a thief.
And there's my old clock that might have chicken pox.
Hey it's a new cookie that I think is a rental.
Hey there's only one thing left. Dust bunnies that I would call
Rust Buddies because everybody is having a good time, so I'll
have to have them rhyme.
By Ivana G. (fourth grader)

MY DESK

All my work goes in my desk and usually never returns.
My folders are filled with paper and packets that make my desk messy.
My books are here and there also everywhere that you could imagine.
All my toys are down and around that keep my desk fun.
All the colors in my desk explode like a rainbow lighthouse colors that come from my colored pencils too, but what makes my desk sparkle are all of the markers.
I have about ten rulers in my desk that are everywhere. The scissors sometimes surface. The glue squirts almost everywhere where there's paper and folders and my toys too. My notebooks are filled with doodles. The colors that are the most important thing in my desk are my loose little papers that roam around my desk and surface when I clean my desk out.
By Isabella R. (fourth grader)

AUTUMN

Crunch, scrunch go the leaves.
Whirl, swirls go the leaves.
Candy corn, Indian corn, sweet corn galore.
Cackling witches, dancing skeletons decorate the houses.
Footballs fly through the air.
Children giggling and playing
Smells of nutmeg, cinnamon and pumpkin pie
Come as the wind blows your hair.
Geese honking as they fly in a V-shape formation,
As they fly you sense the winter is coming.
By Anna K. (fourth grader)

COMMUNITY SONG

Our Song is a secret garden full of green
Gently moving spirits of those who have
Gone before, moving the branches
Back and forth in the garden's center.
Centrally located, an oak provides shade,
Shelter and nourishment for other living beings.
As beautiful and fragrant as roses in bloom,
Our song looks and feels like soft, smooth velvet
Working together as one.
Our song sounds as busy as pollinating bees
And squirrels quickly gathering nuts.
Sharing ideas and working together as fast
And furiously as popcorn popping.
Our song dreams of bright, warm summer days
And the dark blue of a refreshing lake.
One night, dreams take us to the magical
Places we've explored together.
Our song depends upon honesty, warm greetings,
And welcoming hearts!
By Mary Groesch

THE GOLDEN TREE

The golden tree standing brighter
Than all the others brown.
Yellowish leaves reflecting the sun
On a crisp autumn day.
Around the tree, birds fly
Searching for a place to land.
As the wind blows,
A spot is revealed for the birds to rest.
After a short time the birds fly away,
And a squirrel climbs up the trunk.
It gets colder as the leaves
Float to the ground.
Another squirrel climbs
To the safety of the tree.
The graceful tree standing strong is a perfect home,
And sometimes a good one for us too.
Standing strong,
Protecting others,
Graceful in difficult times,
Are Lessons Learned from a Tree.
By Rebecca G. and Nicole U. (fourth graders)

I included a poem of my own, "The Ebb and Flow of the Ocean's Tide," for two reasons. First, I believe that as a teacher, I have to be able to model what it means to be a writer and a learner. I need to understand what an enormous challenge it may be for some to write poetry. How would I have any idea without being a writer myself? Secondly, the poem serves as a metaphor for my own philosophy of teaching. I believe that each day when children come into my classroom, something magical may occur that day within our community. It is the ebb and flow of the tide. There is a greater power beyond the tide, but with the tide and sand in concert, wonderful things may happen. I can prepare and provide opportunities, and if a child is ready, then he or she can explore a tidal pool, dive beneath the surface of the water, or even discover a pearl. Each day, a teacher and his or her students have the opportunity for exploration and discovery in all areas of learning. When missteps happen, as inevitably they do, the tide washes away the footprints, and the next day everyone begins anew with a "clean slate."

THE EBB AND FLOW OF THE OCEAN'S TIDE
By Mary Groesch

The ocean's tide allows for exploration and renewal.
Everyday smooth driftwood floats gently to shore.
An opportunity to build sandcastles,
Slay dragons,
And travel to faraway lands.
Constantly nourishing tidal pools
Hidden among the rocks where
Starfish and sponges may abound.
High tide erases footprints providing a clean slate.
Encouraging some to explore beneath the surface,
Discovering the coral colonies and exotic fish.
Rare occasions when a pearl is discovered nestled inside a shell
Saltwater and sand, in concert,
Provide endless possibilities
For creativity and discovery.

I hope you enjoy these impressive poems written by fourth and fifth graders, nine- and ten-year-old children. Sometimes I would have the children write about their families as we needed to get to know each other better, and it always was an important part of our family history unit. The elements are the same; each poet needs have a line about each member of the family, including pets.

Chapter 3

EXPLORING OUR FIVE SENSES

As human beings we use our five senses—touch, sight, smell, hearing, and taste—to perceive the world. Using our senses we can tell if our favorite meal is going to be served or if we like the music playing on the radio. Before writing, it is important to sharpen the writers' senses. For sight, you can put twenty to twenty-five different, interesting objects on a tray and cover them with a cloth. Once the time limit is decided upon, you can take the cloth away and allow the children to look at the objects and try and memorize them. For those students who remember most of them, ask them if they had a system developed to aid in memorization. It can be a challenge to describe the sense of hearing through writing. Sometimes it is the setting that is described so well that the reader says to himself or herself, "I know what that sounds like!"

Here are some poems that focus on the senses of tasting and hearing.

WATERMELON

Pop, pop, faster, louder
Creamy, crispy, fresh and clean,
Its lovely colors of red and green
With slippery dark black seeds.
Everything my taste buds need,
A delicious summer time treat.
It's something good to eat,
Watermelon.
By Lisi W. (fourth grader)

MICROWAVE POPCORN

Pop, pop, faster, louder.
The buzzer rings.
I empty the steaming bag into a bowl.
Add butter, gently sprinkle salt.
Now it's ready to eat. Yummy treat!
By Ray W. (fourth grader)

POETRY TREE

My tree, my own pine tree,
Which I planted four years ago,
Is behind my house in my backyard.
Four years ago it was two feet tall,
And now it's about as tall as me.
When I'm next to it, it smells like fresh flowers.
I visit it every day.
When I look at it, it reminds me of four years ago when I played with it.
It's very special to me.
It's not like any other tree.
By Nell V. (fourth grader)

LOLLIPOP

So much depends upon
A lollipop.
When I lick it I
Cannot stop.

When I go to bed.
To rest my head.
I lick my lollipop.

It falls on the floor.
And goes splat!
I see its shattered
Into pieces.
So I cry out, "I want Reeses."
By Sammy D. (fourth grader)

SALSA

Salsa is delicious creamy mouth-watering
Goodness that is what salsa brings.

It has a wonderful sensation.
I just can't let go of when
My taste buds eat it.
They go ding, ding, ding!
It makes me want to go to bed.

This mouth-watering goodness,
I always hope it brings
Because when I think about it
My taste buds sing.
By Samantha S. (fourth grader)

Games are a good way of introducing and practicing the senses of seeing, touching, and smelling. Ask your class to help you. For smelling, walk from child to child, letting him or her get a good whiff of what you have. Children need to write down their guesses on a piece of paper you provide. After you get through all of the senses, it is time to take a closer look. Reveal an interesting object, and discuss it with your class. What is the most telling characteristic of the object? What quality do you think of when you see this object? Some of these activities might be done cooperatively with each group changing places once everyone has had a chance to smell or touch it. Also, give children a chance to use their powers of observation. Before writing, some may want to observe and record their findings in their poetry notebook.

The following are poems that focus on the last three senses:

THE BEACH

At the beach I am free.
I feel the sand go through my toes.
I hear the waves crash against the shore.
I touch the smooth rocks before the tide comes back.
I watch the seagulls cut through the sky and
Watch the imaginative line.
I smell the ocean spray and feel it on my face.
And now I'm home.
By Faith D. (fourth grader)

SNAKE ROAD

Climbing up the pole I was scared.
But I knew there was just air up there.
Step by step afraid to look down,
So far away was the flat ground.
Inch by inch across the narrow line.
I really didn't feel at all fine.
Leaning back parallel to the ground
I found myself safely going back down.
By Molly H. (fourth grader)

Drama games are an important means of learning about the different parts of speech. I participated in two classes of theater games for teachers at the Piven Workshop in Evanston, Illinois. Another resource is renowned English dramatist Dorothy Heathcote's book about creating an ongoing drama. In Heathcote's summer course I learned how to create a whole class drama experience. The teachers were gardeners working in an 16th[h] century English estate during the time of Beowulf. We also experienced what it was like to be ship wreaked on a deserted island.

Divide children into groups of six to eight for the group games. One game I found useful was "Statue." Participants come to the stage one by one. They have to remain connected to each other through touch, and their face should always be in full view of the audience. You could say, "Make a bridge." Then you could say, "Click," and then say a kind of bridge or an adjective. Possible words include: draw, stone, toll, Golden Gate, wooden, rickety, and new. Hearing the word, the group makes a quick change. It is important for them to realize that the changes are quick and the construct is not literal. "Machine" is another useful game. The group should have six to eight participants. One by one, each person comes to the stage, assumes a position, and makes a repetitive movement and sound. Machines range from real ones like a blender to metaphorical ones like a "party machine."

Using the "Explore Your Senses" as a prewriting activity, you are going to write a poem about your senses and "magic senses." Use the actual senses to explore your world through specific, concrete detail (literal image). The magic senses are explored through metaphor. Here's an example of a literal image: "With my hands I can feel the rocky soil in my grandmother's garden and the cool of her wedding ring." Here is a magic sense: "With my magic hands I can touch the soft memories of my grandmother and the broken music of the moonlight." Supply a journal page for senses. Then ask the children to record all of the nouns, adverbs, and verbs they see or hear (depending upon the sense). Then children may write down phrases. Example: "Rustling leaves, pulled loose from their branches, dance wildly upon the path." This journal serves as a prewriting activity or planner so that they may write poems when they return to school.

Here are some models for the students:

> My eyes
> See the beautiful colors of
> The rainbow after the rain.
>
> My magic eyes
> Can see the color
> Of the flower's heart.
>
> With my ears I can hear the brakes
> Of the cars on the street.
>
> With my magic ears
> I can hear fish moving in the sea.

Below I made a copy of a worksheet that I put in the camp journal as a planner:

With my hands I can feel or touch _____

With my magic hands I can feel or touch _____

My hands can feel _____

My magic hands I can feel _____

My eyes can see _____

My magic eyes can see _____

With my tongue I can taste _____

With my magic tongue I can _____

My ears can hear or listen to _____

With my magic ears I can hear or listen to _____

With my nose I can smell _____

With my magic nose I can smell _____

Listening to some peaceful instrumental music may provide your students a chance to write a poem about what is important to them. Imagine it is just you and the sky and the stars in the wondrous environment containing trees. What would you want to say to the world? Tell your heart's song. This is one of the suggestions I included in a camp journal where students were going to spend the night. Another journal activity was to discuss Wallace Stevens' "Thirteen Ways of Viewing a Blackbird." After discussing the short stanzas, the children will then write poem about how people may view them in thirteen ways. Here are some examples of the children's poems:

With my hands i can feel the grass.
With my magic hands I can feel the grasses' feelings.
My eyes can see the rainbow.
My magic eyes can see the pot of gold at the end of the rainbow.
With my tongue I can taste the food in front of me.
With my magic tongue I can taste all of the food.
With my ears I can hear the wind.
With my magic ears I can hear the wind talking to me.
With my nose I can smell animals.
With my magic nose I identify the different kinds of animals.
By Lauren D. (fourth grader)

MY SPECIAL PLACE

My special tree is my special place.
I can swing on the branches all day and look out at the peach
smooth sandy beaches and the calm blue lake.
One day we all packed up the car and left for the winter.
It was a long winter with lots of snow.
Finally, it was spring and we started our long drive back to the
summer house.
When we pulled up to the door I raced out of the car, by acci-
dent shutting the door on my brother, and ran behind the house
and up the tree. "Dinner" My mom called out the door to me. I
walked inside.
Later that night there was a big storm.
In the morning I looked at the poor tree that had to stand there
All night in the rain.
I touched its dark wet bark with my finger.
Its roots burrow through the thick coarse soil strongly,
Growing bigger every day.
Its leaves slowly fall gliding through the wind.
Its branches bend and sway gleaming through the sunlight.
My tree survives the massive winds, rain, and lightning.
Its bark slowly breaks off through the dense storms.
The scar from the lightning becomes permanent
Like the Indian art.
The art reminds me of the Indians of long ago.
By Karinn S. (fourth grader)

Chapter 4

TREES, TREES, AND MORE TREES

The first section consists of poems written about different places, environments, and biomes in our world. Geography is key a part of my classroom and is integrated into every part of the curriculum. Progressive teaching has at least a dozen characteristics, one of which is the integrated nature of the social studies units. Social studies is a marriage of history and geography (time and place). National Geographic created the Five Themes of Geography in the late 1980s and is one way of enabling people to see the relationships between place, absolute and relative location, region, movement (how people, goods, and ideas move from place to place), and human/environment interaction (how do we affect the earth and how does the earth affect us?). It's important for children to understand through modeling, their studies, and activities. I normally introduce children to the five themes using picture books. Then, in cooperative groups, children are given a stack of books, and they need to divide them by the main theme each book represents. Critical for children is to have the five themes visually represented on a wall or bulletin board within the classroom.. For fourth and fifth graders, a population study with materials from the Population Reference

Bureau (based in Washington, DC) is another link to understanding the big concepts in social studies.

The two main biomes in our part of the state are the woodlands and the prairie. In earlier years, we worked with the Cook County Forest Preserve to help restore a prairie. Once our work was completed, we could arrange field trips to the Chicago Botanic Garden throughout the year to learn about each of these biomes. Writing to your state should provide you with key information for your biomes.

For the woodlands, I received pamphlets on the woodland mammals, woodland products, and tree types and the related vocabulary. The Illinois endangered mammals are gray bat, Indiana bat, eastern wood bat, and the white-tailed jackrabbit. Threatened animals are river otter, bobcat, golden mouse, and rice rat. Animals of the past are elk, black bear, timber wolf, cougar, marten, and fisher. White ash, black oak, black cherry, eastern cottonwood, and American elm are just five of the roughly twenty-four different kinds of trees found in Illinois woodlands. We get an amazing amount of products that we need from trees. We get cordwood, poles, piles, posts, logs stumps, gums, foliage, nuts, and fruit. Trees give people many benefits: watershed protection, soil stabilization, natural beauty, wind control, recreation, and products. Making sure children understand the basic concepts enables them to glean the most from the seasonal activities done in the woodlands.

In the fall, examine the environmental factors that affect the woodlands. Brainstorm factors that affect plants in the classroom and outside, and sort into biotic (from living organisms) and abiotic. Make a chart for reference. Review how trees grow and what affects their growth. The Nature Scope issue on trees discusses tree rings. Read the rings and consider environmental factors that affect growth such as: drought, heavy rainfall, fire, insect infestation, and building next to the woodlands. Estimate the height of the tree and guess its age. Look at how trees live by reviewing photosynthesis; show transpiration by placing baggies over cacti versus other plants; and watch bulb roots grow in water. What are the environmental factors? Activities children may do on their first trip include adopting a tree and making observations about the kinds of leaves such as alternate, opposite leaves, simple and compound leaves, and lobed and toothed leaves. A helpful book, worth purchasing for each of the groups, is _Tree Finder: A Manual for the Identification of Trees_ by May Theilgaard Watts. Also, send small groups to prepared places to make observations. Last, evaluate where the garbage has gone. Categorize the trash into four groups: non-biodegradable, biodegradable, non-recyclable, and recyclable.

In the winter, animals that stay in the cold weather have adapted to the conditions of snow, ice, and cold. Some animals migrate (from hundreds of miles to a few hundred yards). Animals hibernate or enter periods of dormancy during the coldest parts of winter. Some animals may remain active, feeding as best as they can. Teach the vocabulary for twigs: terminal bud, lateral bud, leaf scar, lenticels, vein of bundle scar, bud scale scar, and pith. Give each small group some twigs to examine and to identify their characteristics. Early on, teach children how to use a thermometer, and give them practice predicting the temperature before it is measured. For their seasonal walk through the forest, they will notice significant differences. Children should notice how things have changed since autumn. Compare and contrast the changes in the canopy, understory, shrubs, and forest floor between the fall and the winter trips. On their individual walks, students should make temperature predictions and record actual temperature. If there is snow, they should predict the snow depth and then take measurements. Have them describe the weather conditions. How do they think the current weather conditions are affecting the woodland animals? Sketch the view and include all the layers of the forest, the animals and the signs of life that you have observed.

Spring slowly transforms the woodlands. Before the canopy has its green appearance, the first of the spring flowers bloom. Discuss the importance of human relationships with forests. Before visiting the woodlands for a third time, ask students to create wildlife want ads. Have students work in small groups comparing and contrasting the woodlands to a city. Pass out a sheet of wildflowers that bloom during the month of May. Helpful teacher resources include Ranger Rick's *Nature Scope*, especially "Trees are Terrific," "Wading Into Wetlands," and "Birds, Birds, Birds!"

Here are some examples of nature writing:

THREE OAKS HILL

Three Oaks Hill standing strong
Against the world.
In the late autumn
Rising mist makes the trees
Appear as dark outstretched limbs
Worshipping the sky.
Monuments emerging from the gray
Mist of the arboretum.
By Mary Groesch

FOREST

Green leaves and grass with dew,
Golden sunlight breaking through,
Birds singing on branches
Sweet smells of multi-colored flowers,
Pine needles covered in sweet sap
Prick me as I walk by.
As if they want me to stay.
By Claire A. (fourth grader)

FALLING LEAF

First it falls from the tree,
Falls down with other leaves
Crunchy and jumping off the ground
Dances beautifully without a sound,
Or sits quietly so you can see,
But it always starts from a tree.
By Elise D. (fourth grader)

A PATH

I look out my window and on the other side of the river I see
A path through the woods flanked by trees.
As creatures crawl in every direction.
You can walk on the crisp autumn leaves,
Crunching with each step.
The leaves are purple, brown, red and yellow.
The ramble is a sight to see with all those trees
So sturdy and tall.
The path spreads long and wide before me,
Just like my life.
By Ms. Groesch's fourth-grade class

BONFIRE

Bonfire, bonfire burning bright.
Sparks ignite the empty night.
Wondrous, mysterious sight!
Shadows dancing with the path
Showing the outstretched arms of the trees.
Spreading long and wide before me,
Just like my life!
By Mary Groesch

SPECIAL TREE

I used to go up to my special tree
Seeing it would make my heart beat with glee
That tree was tall with its arms open wide.
Was always itself with nothing to hide.
Its arms so big calling me
So that I could come in and hide.
It has bushes that block the path.
It has stinging bees buzzing around the flowers.
It has poison ivy hidden in the bushes.
It has sprinklers that shower you
When you don't want to get wet.
When you come to a fork in the path,
Choose one way and carry on.
By Allegra G. (fourth grader)

ARIZONA

A spicy smell fills the air.
The sky is clear.
The ground feels hot.
Taste the sand blowing into your mouth.
Water! Water!
It was too dry.
Hear the dehydrated wind
Rushing past your ear,
Can you hear it?
It's calling you.
By Kristen B. (fourth grader)

TREE GLORY

Many things remind me of trees.

I love trees because of their beauty and how they help us.

Someone who makes your garden so pretty that it showers its beauty on your house.

Trees, even though they are so beautiful, there is so much more to them.

A tree is even more beautiful on the inside. When a tree is cut you can see its history.

Count the rings of how long they have lived, hopefully a long helpful life.

Trees always such a dream. YOU can never truly own a tree because its beauty stands out, and says, "I am my own and I help the earth with my soul."

And you can see, hug a tree, just like me.

By Isabella R. (fourth grader)

Chapter 5

THE WORLD AND US

I was fortunate to be trained by National Geographic in their teacher initiative program, which began in the late 1980s. My state and a neighboring state were heavily involved in training teachers. I was lucky to have approximately twenty years of training and travelling. National Geographic created the concept of the five themes of geography: location, place, region, movement, and human/environment interaction. These five themes have helped countless students understand the world better. I had taught at two international schools for five years in Lima, Peru, and Santiago, Chile. When I learned about the five themes, I was able to better understand where I had lived and worked better. *Location* refers to where things are located on the earth's surface. Location is both absolute (latitude and longitude) and approximate, such as living north of Chicago on the shores of Lake Michigan. *Place* is what makes your location special and different from any other. What makes it special? *Region* is what your place has in common with other places in the area. This may refer to the same geographic or cultural area. *Movement* is how people, goods, and ideas move from one place to another. Lastly, *human-environmental interaction* is how the earth affects us and how we affect the earth. Geography was a part of almost every social studies, science or literature lesson I taught.

Here are some examples of geographic poems:

SEASONS

Winter is freezing; winter is cold.
It brings the chills down your back.
Playing in the snow is so much fun,
And soon comes the sun.

Spring is happy a new fawn is born.
The brooks are melted, and so is the sun.
The robins are chirping and
Fill the meadow with wonderful sounds.

Summer is really warm
Like a boiling pot of water.
The flowers are finally growing
And so are the blossoms on the trees.

Fall is windy; it's so much fun.
Jumping in the leaves, red, yellow, brown,
September through November,
And then the first snowflake appears.
By Rebecca G., Brayden M., and Kelly Z. (fourth graders)

The grass waving in the wind,
And my feet sloshing through the muck.
Fearful my shoes will be stuck in the mud.
Although it's now sunny.
It's time to return home.
By Emelia S. (fourth grader)

YELLOW IGUANAS

Yellow iguanas, spiny from the crown down.
Yellow iguanas living in dark caves,
Lifeless lava fields of the Galapagos.
Coloring varies from island to island,
From yellow to black, orange to dark green.
Living on the coastal fringe of the Pacific.
By Nicole U. (fourth grader)

AT THE BEACH

I hear the ocean,
I feel the sand,
I feed the seagulls with my hand.
I smell that beautiful fresh sea air
And the wind blowing, I stroke my hair.
I go to a lovely place for lunch,
Many people waiting in one big bunch.
I sniff in a wonderful smell.
Soon my taste buds are watering.
Oh, I'm so hungry!
Joyfully I go to sit down
When our table's ready.
I see a little kid playing with his toy,
For I want to remember this magnificent place.
This has been wonderful day.
The young whelp curls up to dream without peep.
By Samantha S. (fourth grader)

RAINFOREST

The sound of rain hitting the treetops in the rainforest.
You can hear the rain, but you can't feel it.
The canopy forms an umbrella.
The monkeys swing from branch to branch.
The snakes slither on the forest floor.
The ants carry their dinner on their backs following one after
another.
The birds swoop over the forest.
The slight rustle through the trees
And out comes a jaguar on the hunt for food.
Even in the heat of the day.
The rainforest is full of life.
The snakes slither on the forest floor.
The ants carry their dinner on their backs,
Following one after another.
The birds swoop over the forest.
The slight rustle through the trees
And out comes a jaguar
On the hunt for food.
Even in the heat of the day
The rainforest is full of life.
By Faith D. (fourth grader)

WAITING

I sit on the bench of life and wait.
I wait for the next person.
The next child to make the next move,
To take on the next challenge.
I have so many dreams,
But not the courage to share them
In the line of the world.
I am always moving back one space,
Avoiding being first in line.
I now have the courage.
I am the last man standing in line.
It is my turn to make a change.
By Lisi W. (fourth grader)

ACROSS THE COUNTRY TO FIND THE LAND OF WONDERS I ROAM

Between two mountains
Below, the possibilities it lies.
Before I knew it, I stepped into a hole
Slid through and across it,
I was somewhere I didn't know. Where could I be?
The place I would find wonders or answers
Along a bookshelf lay magical books.
"I was finally there!"
By Blair S. (fourth grader)

Between the back by the big window, a table stands
Where I can make anything in the world:
A dog, a robin, a rabbit.
Bubbles are round.
I feel the world in my hands.
Fold, cut, tape, glue and paint.
It will always stand.
By Kelly Z. (fourth grader)

SNOW

The tracks of the doe do
Hippity Hop!
Bears hibernate sleepy and slow
Roses have a satin gown.
The world is a blur of white.
Smoke swirls out of the chimney.
The snowman smiles at me.
The icicles hang from the gutters.

The children skate on the lake that
Is cold as the wind.
The night owl sits in a big black nest.
In the cold you can hear people saying
"Happy New Year!"
By Kip W. (fourth grader)

BUBBLES

Bubbles, bubbles you blow.
They pop!
Bubbles are round.
Bubbles, bubbles you blow.
They pop!
Bubbles are round.
And when they burst,
They make a sound,
Pop! Pop! Pop!
They never stop.
They float up to the very top.
Bubbles are round.
And when they burst
They make a sound
And, they make a sound,
Pop! Pop! Pop!
They never stop.
They float up to the very top.
They make the noise
Plop, Plop, Plop!
They make a sound,
Pop! Pop! Pop!
They make the noise
Plop, Plop, Plop!
By Nell V. (fourth grader)

THE LEAF

A leaf is soft and smooth,
With all of its green grooves.
The wind blows it around.
Dancing in the air before
It lands on the ground.
It's staring up at the tree
Where it once began.
By Sammy D. (fourth grader)

FORESTS

Tall green trees with strong brown trunks,
Sounds of birds singing are everywhere.
The taste of leaves greet me in the air,
Stinging of bees on my arms,
All wrapped up in fragrant scent.
By Allegra G. (fourth grader)

THE SUMMER SUN

Hot summer sun beating down on everyone,
Making smiles come to faces.
As children build sand castles and dig holes in the wet moist sand
Discovering sea glass, shells, discarded tires,
Treasures of the sea.
Small children enjoy swimming, snorkeling, jet skiing, and tubing!
The sun provides warmth and fun for everyone.
By Annie S. (fifth grader)

Chapter 6

ALL KINDS OF ANIMALS

Animals are a key element of any ecosystem. The first part of the animal section relates to pets because children, and many adults as well, experience a deep connection with their family pet. In preparing to write, ask the children to brainstorm all of their feelings, images, and memories they have of the animal. This section will reveal what the writer feels before starting to write the initial draft. What comes to mind when they think of their animal? Is it a friend or someone to talk to about important subjects? Does the child experience comfort stroking the animal's fur? The focus of the poem may be a comparison of the pet to something else not obviously apparent to the reader. In the pet poems, you will see that pets are playmates, trusted confidantes, and very important family members.

Research is an important part of any written piece. Children naturally see the importance when they are writing a nonfiction report. For the animal poetry, it is important to understand all of the fact-gathering information about the specific animal. A sheet could be provided with common names for male and female animals, the name of the young or juveniles, the common name given for the sound the animals make (if any), the group noun where applicable, and the name of an artificial shelter for the animals.

Once they have chosen their animal, the writers may highlight the information about their animals and then write about their predator and prey relationships. Children should explain how the animal contributes to and benefits its ecosystem.

Here are some animal poems:

ABBY, THE COLOR OF LOVE

Your loud purr was so brave and strong.
I could listen to it all day long.
You were important and special to me.
When I would see you my heart would jump with glee.
You were so very smart.
I remember the cat food in the cart.
Your soft fuzzy head was calming to pet.
I will always remember you in my heart and my head.
By Alina T. (fourth grader)

I start weeping now
Remembering my puppy
Who died last August.
By Cam L. J. (fourth grader)

My good friend Shadow
A bundle of energy,
Never seems to sleep.
By Ray W. (fourth grader)

ELLA

My precious little puppy dog
Very cute and chews a log.
Sounds very loud, "bark, bark, bark,"
Plops down and makes a big thud
Woof! Woof!
She is hungry for food
Or needs to go potty.
Oh, I need my big Béarnaise Mountain Dog.
Ella scratches the couch; scratch, scratch.
She doesn't like water; splash, splash.
But she loves the soft fluffy snow
My playmate Ella.
By Griffin K. (fourth grader)

MADDY

Maddy was a golden lab,
But she was man's best friend.
When I was five
She was about my size.
We used to lie side by side
And watch TV.
Whenever she saw mom and me
Maddy wagged her tail excitedly.
Loved getting her belly rubbed
She slept in the family room.
Sadly, she left us far too soon.
By Johnny H. (fourth grader)

KELSEY

Lying in the summer sun is so, so, so hot,
Except when you sit right under a tree.
When you are all rested and cool
Come outside and play with me—
A little soccer or tennis,
Pick flowers or go swimming.
Come on you little happy face!
Let's pick a cherry or two.
Come on you little happy face!
Let's look at the moon and stars tonight.
It's supposed to be very nice.
Come on, let's go and ask the other three in the family.
Come, show them all of your love.
Show them all your stuff—
Your strength, power and all of you.
By Annie S. (fifth grader)

COOKIE JAR

What's in the jar?
Is it a candy bar or
Does it have lots of cookies?
What is in the jar?
The dog longingly gazes
At the jar on the counter.
By Sammy D. (fourth grader)

NOW THAT YOU ARE GONE

I miss you each and every day.
At night I look for your sleeping face
And wonder where you are.

Now that you are gone
I wonder if I will ever have another
Beautiful soul to love and call my own?

We were always connected like salt and pepper.
I know that I will always miss you
Now that you are gone.
By Mary Groesch

HAVE YOU HEARD A DOG BARK?

Have you ever heard a dog
In a noisy park?
Hear them bark in the house
At a quiet white mouse?
We love our dogs,
Even though they can be very
Annoying.
By Gunnar L. (fourth grader)

WILSON

Black, thick coat with creamy brown eyes,
Smells so many unknown scents
I'm never surprised.
His flat, pink tongue licks me silly,
I can't help saying, "ENOUGH Willy."
Annoys us at dinner, wanting a bite,
Barks all night, which is not all right.
By Cooper M. (fourth grader)

THAT ELEPHANT

That elephant just standing there,
Not moving, silent and still.
That elephant is a fake!
I can tell because it is different.
Its trunk isn't as long as others.
Its ears are too big and floppy.
How weird is that?
By Johnny H. (fourth grader)

WHEN THE MOON STARTS TO RISE

Cricket gets on his tie,
And grabs his violin
That's when the chorus will begin
By Claire A. (fourth grader)

OTTERS

Otters are the cutest creatures,
They seem to play all day.
However, they are also sleepers
And stop their play
So they can eat, but after that
They return to their fun.
It seems that in the otter's world
Nothing *ever* gets done.
A rock becomes a play toy.
A stream becomes a place for tag.
Those that are fast get away,
But others often lag.
"Tag! You're it!"
Then in otter talk they say:
"The sun is setting, it's time to sleep."
Back to home in the side of the bank,
Mother's preparing to sleep.
The young whelp curls up to dream without a peep.
By Adam W. (fifth grader)

The Queen dog sits in her throne and
In her mouth sits a big bold bone.
On her head is her fabulous crown
With jewels going all around.
On her face is a grin so wide and
With great pride.
She eats her treats all day long,
And according to her kingdom,
With jewels going all around.
On her face is a grin so wide and
With great pride.
She eats her treats all day long,
And according to her kingdom,
She's never ever wrong.
She get pampered in bed and
Usually gets her nails manicured red.
By Anna W. (fourth grader)

CLOUDED LEOPARD

The clouded Leopard is an elegant creature
While hunting as silent as mid-winter snow,
Pristine in the silence.
It approaches its prey without a sound.
A more beautiful creature was never seen,
Southeast Asia.
By Adam W. (fifth grader)

DOG TO PUPPY

Life's not always been off the leash.
It's been being a good dog,
Not being brought into a big room
Full of cages of overwhelming barks
And sad faces.
Always remember how far we've come,
But don't give up.
By Faith D. (fourth grader)

On a lily pad
Sits silently, until it spies
A tasty treat.
By Elise D. (fourth grader)

CORMORANT

As sleek as a Cheetah,
As graceful as a Falcon,
As elegant as a Clouded Leopard
Yet as plain as a Crow
A fisher by nature,
In many ways it is a flying harpoon
It thinks_*them*_a good meal.
By Adam W. (fifth grader)

MOSQUITO

This will make you itch,
The constant buzzing around your ears
And the endless swatting,
And the red bumps.
When you think about it,
It's really quite funny to
Observe an insect drinking
Your blood like lemonade.
By Sammy D. (fourth grader)

Chapter 7

COLOR POEMS

Collect some books from the library on color. One that comes to my mind is Bill Martin's *Brown Bear, Brown Bear*. Explain how adjectives describe nouns or pronouns (How tall? How quiet?). Make lists for your class with unusual names for colors. Here is a start: rose (red), indigo (blue), azure (blue), rust, copper, bronze, topaz (yellow), ivory (white), obsidian (black), coal (black), ebony (black), emerald (green), ruby (red), sienna (brown), flame, (violet), lush (pink), bruise, moss (green) (purple), mauve, amethyst, clay, lavender (purple), frost, midnight, (plum), lemon, sapphire (blue), turquoise, (blue) amber, smoke, charcoal (dark gray), jade (green), olive (green), brick, poppy, sage, opal, crimson (red), slate gray, dove gray, and ash gray. Another great book is *Living Color*, which focuses on all of the incredible colors nature offers us. My favorite color book I use for the poetry model is *Hailstones and Halibut Bones*. Each poem is titled by a color—such as "What is White?"—and every poem mentions what nouns, emotions, and feelings are created by the color.

After the children select a color, they need to make lists. What does the color remind them of? What feelings do they have when they think of this color? What kind of a person is described with certain colors? Reinforce that colors are adjectives because they describe nouns (person, place or thing). Ask the children to select a color and list all the things that they think of when they think of that color. For example, "Black is the hat of the Halloween witch who sweeps through the sky/ Black is also the little black dress of the lady who attends an opening gala." Remind students that adjectives describe and make nouns and pronouns interesting. There are different kinds of adjectives; those that describe the color of the noun/pronouns, the shape of the noun, the texture, and its number.

Below are some poems that children have written. The poems vary in complexity.

The color of that bright blue sea,
Soothingly, shining back at me.
I love the beautiful sparkling rocks
For when I look at that wonderful dock.
This is a place I'll never forget,
For that bright shining sun
Will always be lit.
By Emelia S. (fourth grader)

ORANGE

Orange is a color of a beautiful sunset,
Or Jack-O-Lantern waiting to be lit.
Then you see a big, tall tree,
With every orange leaf in the world.
Seeing it makes me relax,
New and old every day,
Farewell outside for now I must go.
Although the night is blue
I still feel the orange glow.
Or Jack-O-Lantern waiting to be lit.
Orange moon shines warm and cold,
New and old every day,
Farewell outside for now I must go.
Although the night is blue
I still feel the orange glow.
By Stephany P. (fourth grader)

PINK

Pink is like a flower or a Valentine.
It's like a lollipop with a pink design
Or a red color like a pink rose
Held in a woman's bouquet at a sad farewell.
Every color can be expressed in different emotions.
Blue can be an ice color that can be sad.
Red can be happy as in the rainbow.
Pink is a color with a nice shade of red.
By Brayden M. (fourth grader)

WHAT IS BLUE?

Blue is the color of sadness
For some people,
But for me, it is a very happy color.
Blue is color that fills me with joy,
And that is what is my favorite color.
The best mood to be in and just
Seeing it makes me relax.
Blue raspberry candy so sweet
Keeps me occupied for thirty minutes.
When I finish my mouth is blue,
A reminder of the sweet taste lingering.
Blue is color that fills me with joy,
And that is what is my favorite color.
By Tommy W. (fourth grader)

WHAT IS PINK?

Sweet pink is the twinkling light that ripples
Through the sunset when its dusk.
Pink is the frosting on a birthday cake
You put on after it went into the oven to bake.
Pink is the bow that ties up a little girl's hair that
You have to tie up nicely with lots of care.
Pink is the color of your fat eraser
that takes care of the mistake you left there.
Pink thinks she's perfect, but she's really not.
When the other colors knock on her door, it'll be locked.
By Anna W. (fourth grader)

YELLOW

Yellow is hot buttered popcorn that cools in your mouth.
When it's dark the happiness of a firefly brightens up the darkness.
It makes you yellow inside.
They are the daffodils that bloom in spring.
Yellow is the round sun or stars that brightens up the universe.
By Lucy E. (fourth grader)

RED

Red is the embarrassment when you forget your homework.
Your face turns red.
Red is when you are sweating really hard.
Red is like a rocket lifting off into space.
Red is your blood flowing through your veins.
Red can be many things, but you get my point,
It could be a red sweater or a red house.
Red is like a valentine
My dad gives my mom to say, "I love you."
By Makhoul C. (fourth grader)

BLACK

Shadow is a sweet, black lab,
Who is my great friend.
Black is the color of her coat.
Shadow has a room of her own.
Full of toys, cushions, water bowl
And a food dish.
Returning home I eat a snack
And we play together.
Throwing tennis balls
She bounces after them.
In her mouth she thinks she OWNS the balls.
I wrestle with her
For those balls
So that I can throw them
For her again.
By Ray W. (fourth grader)

Chapter 8

DREAMS, MAGICAL CREATURES, SPECIAL PLACES, AND PEOPLE

C hildren love to use their imaginations to think about fantasy and
to dream about the future. Many of them have their special places
where they go to think.

Here are poems about their dreams and special places:

DREAM CATCHER

My life-long dream
Is to be a basketball player
On an NBA team.
The Houston Rockets is my choice.
If I am given a voice,
I love making the shots
And being the person on the spot,
Who makes the winning shot.
My life-long dream is to be
A basketball player on an NBA team.
By Ray W. (fourth grader)

MY DREAM

I have a dream unlike any other.
It took me a long time to discover.
Sometimes dreams can fly away like a winged bird,
Flying away day to day.
So hold onto your dream.
Don't let it swim away like a fish
In a raging stream.
Don't let go of your precious dream.
If you dream to be a dentist,
a pilot or a hockey player,
Hold fast to your dreams so they don't disappear.
By Samantha S. (fourth grader)

MY DREAM

The dreams I have are the world to me.
I get off the bench and play my best.
Life is a field to me.
I make my move.
I spread my wings and fly.
I want to play football for life.
I sit on the bench waiting my turn.
When I play I play my best.
To play for the FALCONS would be a dream come true,
Because it is what I want to do.
Don't let go of your dreams, for if dreams die
Life is an empty room with only a sigh.
By Tommy W. (fourth grader)

THE ATTIC

As I walk into the attic
CREECH goes the floor.
SCREECH goes the door.
As I walk into the attic
My steps get shorter.
So quiet you could even
Hear a needle drop.
I hear a pop!
I run out terrified,
Only then noticing
It was a balloon.
By Sammy D. (fourth grader)

My special place is anywhere safe
Where I can sit and rest.
All I need is a small space
Soft and cozy like a nest.
Only I can fit and no one else can try.
I go there when I'm feeling sad
Or even feeling a little mad,
When I am bored I'll grab a book or
Get some drawing paper from a pad,
But when I get up it falls away
And I continue on with my day.
By Faith D. (fourth grader)

All the way down on the ground
A place so big and round.
If you go closer, a house will appear.
In here is a kitchen, my kind of place.
I make all kinds of food:
Cajun, southwestern, and seafood.
Are you in a good mood?
Well, there's always more.
I'm certainly not a bore.
I hope you can see
This is the place for me.
By Sammy D. (fourth grader)

DREAMS

Dreams are a part of us.
They are sometimes happy and sometimes sad.
Dreams provide everlasting hope.
If you don't dream, your life is surrounded by darkness.
Do dream, you Dreamer and never stop dreaming.
By Griffin K. (fourth grader)

DREAMS

Everybody has dreams.
Some are goals for life.
And some are just when you sleep.
Sometimes you daydream.
A child may dream he's a superhero who can fly.
An adult may dream of flight as an astronaut.
But either way dreams are dreams
And that is the way it is supposed to be.
By Emelia S. (fourth grader)

WHEN I WAS SMALL

When I was small,
My dad was a giant.
He'd pick me up and
Place me on his shoulders.
I felt like I was ten feet tall.
When we wrestled I would fall,
We always had fun together,
But we had to stop sometimes
Or else we'd miss dinner.
By Johnny H. (fourth grader)

MY SPECIAL PLACE

My favorite place is in my yard,
In the plants where the clovers grow.
It is hard to see if I am there,
That is why I love my secret place.
By Allegra G (fourth grader)

Chapter 9

LEARNING PARTS OF SPEECH THROUGH POETRY

E xplain that a sentence contains a verb (action word) and a noun (person, place or thing). Poetry doesn't require sentences and usually just has phrases. However, the poem has to be about something, which is a noun. The more challenging part is finding the right verb to go with the noun. Creating lists of verbs and passing them out to the children as reference sheets helps as does making sure the children understand what the verbs mean. Wonderful resources I've found are the picture books by Ruth Heller. She has written one for each part of speech. *Merry-Go Round* is a book about nouns. *Kites Fly High* is about verbs. There are about a dozen of them about different parts of speech, and they are an invaluable resource when introducing a new concept. As a teacher, you need to look over the list of concepts that you are required to teach and review at your grade level.

Here are words that mean talk or say: croak, bark, grunt, cry out, whisper, dictate, yell, sign, and repeat.

Here are some interesting verbs that mean movement or speech: shatter, nudge, ruffle, slide, strike, melt together, craft, inspire, crack, wrestle, shake, jostle, press, drag, tangle, rescue, meld, sculpt, rust, enliven, scratch, hug, embrace, jolt, bump, push, scrape, rub, join, batter, carve, pierce, hold, squeeze, nestle, bounce, and wrap.

After children have a solid understanding of verbs and nouns, tell them writing would be boring if it were just those parts of speech. The noun/pronoun is what the sentence or phrase is about, and it is referred to as a subject. The simple predicate is the verb and the noun. However, we can add adjectives, words that describe the noun, to make it more interesting. Remind students that adjectives come before the noun in English, but in Spanish the adjectives follow the noun.

Colors are one description that holds constant for every noun. Here is a list of words for color: rose (red), rust, topaz (yellow), coal, ruby, violet, moss, clay, midnight, indigo (blue), copper, ivory (white), ebony (black), sienna (brown), blush (pink), mauve, lavender, plum, azure (blue), bronze, obsidian (black), emerald (green), flame, bruise, amethyst (purple), frost, lemon (yellow), sapphire (blue), smoke, olive, sage, slate gray, turquoise, charcoal (dark gray), brick (red), opal, dove gray, amber (golden), jade (green), poppy, crimson (red), and ash gray.

After learning about prepositions, ask the children to write a prepositional poem to demonstrate their understanding. A preposition is a word that shows a relationship between two or more things. Here is a list of common prepositions: about, above, across, after, against, along, amid, among, anti, around, as, at, before, behind, below, beneath, beside, besides, between, but, by, concerning, considering, despite, down, during, except, excluding, following, for, from, in, inside, into, like, minus, near, of, off, on, onto, opposite, outside, over, past, per, regarding, save, since, than, through, to, toward, under, underneath, unlike, until, up upon, versus, via, with, within, and without.

There are about 150 prepositions in English. Prepositions are used more frequently than other frequent words in the English language. *Of, to,* and *in* are three of the most commonly used words in the English language. Given a list of prepositions, suggest that each line begin with a different preposition until the last line. I usually show a model that is written from an animal's point of view. To write the poem, I will list the prepositions that I plan on using: above, along, amid, across, beneath, and following, Each line begins with a preposition, and then the last line summarizes what has happened.

ABOVE MY HEAD

Above my head,
Along the molding,
Amid the messy contents of my desk,
Across from the set dining room table,
Beneath the Persian rug on the hardwood floor,
Following the scent of the freshly baked cookies,
On the opposite counter near the front door,
Scurried the mouse into the open mouth of a waiting cat.
By Mary Groesch

Another way to practice similes is to supply a pattern:

> As_____as a
> As_____as an
> As_____as
> As_____as
> Is

As angry as a charging bull,
As impatient as a hungry toddler,
As mean as a circling shark,
As crimson as a sunset,
Is when Dad learns my brother totaled his new car.

As the class hears more and more poetry, some things like word choice may become easier. When they become familiar with stanzas as well as poetic devices such as alliteration and onomatopoeia, they will increase their learned vocabulary.

Chapter 10

LEARNING FROM
ESTABLISHED POETS

It is easier to introduce people to metaphor than it is to write a poem metaphorically. Introduce the students to the difference between metaphor and similes. Metaphors and similes are figures of speech that help writers to create vivid and accurate images in their writing. Both figures of speech compare different things. Similes use like or as, while metaphors do not.

I have included the examples I use with the children to introduce them to the concept:

Watermelons are the whales of the summer.
The stars are white fish swimming in the night sea.
My heart is a box that I open and close.
My mind is an open window with the wind blowing in.
The outstretched branches were like fingers grasping the autumn night.
Her smile brightened the room like the sunlight shining through the open window.

The perfect author I've found to use is Emily Dickinson because her poem "Hope is a Thing With Feathers" compares hope to a bird. Throughout the poem, she uses verbs, adjectives, and adverbs to allude to a bird. Children are also introduced to William Carlos Williams, a doctor who wrote poems in his spare time. His poem "This is Just to Say" is a false apology poem. It sounds like a list that he wrote and put on the refrigerator for his wife, and it talks about how he ate the sweet and delicious plums that she was probably saving for breakfast. Another of his poems, "The Red Wheelbarrow," looks at what is important in his neighbor's yard. The first line is "So much depends upon a red wheelbarrow glazed with rain."

Here are some examples of poems modeled after Dickinson and Williams:

THIS IS JUST TO SAY

I let the cat go free
So he could follow me.
He ran off to the town
I couldn't find him then

If you could forgive me,
And give me paper and pen,
I'll work into the night,
I'll find him once again.
By Kirsten B. (fourth grader)

THIS IS JUST TO SAY

I have drunk the
Last soda in the
Refrigerator,

Which you were
Probably saving
For your company.

Forgive me for drinking it,
For it was just sitting there
Calling my name.
It was so cold and delicious.
By Gunnar L. (fourth grader)

SORROW IS A THING WITH RAIN

Sorrow is a thing with rain,
Falling upon people's heads,
Making them droop,
Like flowers in the storm.
And all of the town is dreary.
Happiness can't shine through
The dark storm clouds of sadness,
Comes and cheers you up.
But even so;
Sorrow still clouds our minds
When others feel pain.
By Claire A. (fourth grader)

SERENITY IS THE THING OF A FOREST

Serenity is the thing of a forest
So big and tall standing guard all day
As the leaves fall so smoothly, so calmly;
Just sitting while watching over us.
The trees stand tall with pride in the clearing
With birds chirping all around, all day long.
If a tree is cut down, then you will know that
The serenity will be forever adapted.
Serenity is your own grove of apple trees,
Your calmness, your happiness, greeting you,
Your center is your goodness spreading out,
As the inhabitants of the forest make it their home.
By Rebecca G. (fourth grader)

COMPASSION

Compassion is like a tree
With all the leaves in bloom,
And much space underground
For the roots to roam.
Compassion makes you caring,
Gentle and happy.
Compassion doubles everything in life.
Compassion is like a gift
That it gave you on its own.
Compassion is like the feeling when
You're home sweet home.
By Kirsten B. (fourth grader)

COMPASSION

Compassion is something everyone has,
Even animals share sorrow.
When everyone cares
We'll reach for the sky
And hopefully make a better world.
Compassion is a lost bird with no home.
So let's all give it one…in our hearts.
By Claire A. (fourth grader)

PEACE IS THE THING WITH WATER

A silent moon
Alone in the sand
Saltwater washes your feet.
The first star comes out.
Make a wish!
After all, no one will hear
A peaceful time
There is not a voice
To annoy your hushed daydream.
By Kirsten B. (fourth grader)

EXCITEMENT IS THE THING WITH FIREWORKS

Feel the colors
Blasting into the sky
They might go away, just for a while.

Hear the crowd
Cheering for more.
They want it to keep going
Just like you.

They are going to spark.
They are going to pop.
They will keep going.
They're not going to stop.
Use all their energy.
They are filled with excitement
Just like you.
By Kirsten B. (fourth grader)

Personification means an object or thing (a noun) that has the qualities of a person. Usually two things are being compared in some way ("I'm as mad as a hornet"). For one exercise, each child was given a book written at their reading level to study and to enjoy. The book project was a short report and a poem that they wrote in the style of the poet. I asked students to write poems about an emotion. Treat the emotion as if it were a person. Before writing any format, there has to be planning.

Here is both the planner that a person completed before she wrote about what loneliness meant to her and her poem:

LONELINESS:

Appearance: Color blue, bent over, raggedly clothes, no twinkle in the eyes, stays inside all day, watches TV, activities include mental activities: reading, writing, painting and other work, planning, education, diligent, motivated, hard-working to a fault, lack of balance.

Lives: alone in a place that reflects the travels and experiences of the past life.

Interaction: Doesn't initiate contact once rejected.

Hopes and dreams: to be respected for talents and to travel the world once again.

LONELINESS

Loneliness lives all by herself remembering the friends
That she once had or at least thought she had had.
Often wearing blue, mirroring her face and her mood,
Staying inside all day, for there is no one with whom she may play.
Watching reruns on the television helps her to get away.
Days go by before she bathes and washes her hair,
Wishing that she could be anywhere but where she finds herself.
Once she is rejected or bullied, she will never try to initiate contact again.
Once rejected, always rejected, and no one can cheer her up.
Hoping to be respected as she once was and dreaming of all the
Wonderful, exciting places to visit, anywhere but here.
By Mary Groesch

Here are some student poems:

HORROR

Horror lives in an old gray house down by the edge of the woods.
His spirit scares you and gives you the feeling you aren't going
to make it,
Like when you're alone in a dark house and you hear strange
sounds.
Horror doesn't always enjoy scaring, hearing people scream and
race away.
Sometimes Horror wonders, "Should I open the door and let
Hope in?"
He pauses and keeps the door closed.
By Makhoul C. (fourth grader)

SAD

Sadness is when your heart is too heavy to lug around with you,
So you hunch over,
                Chest facing the ground
                              Because your heart weighs you down.
Maybe a tear or two will fall onto the ground in front of you.
By Mikey W. (fourth grader)

JOY

Joy has many friends.
Joy has shiny white teeth and a smile that never ends.
Joy wakes up early whistling to the birds.
Joy doesn't hide from people and
Always takes the opportunity to meet new friends.
Joy has a beat to the way it walks positive and steady.
Mirroring the happy beat of his heart.
By Brayden M. (fourth grader)

ANGER

Anger is when you don't get what you want or when you just feel
the need to be.
Anger happens the most to selfish, self-centered people because
they always need what they want.

Anger can happen when something is taken from you, but not
just items.
Your dignity or a loved one taken or the right to be free and
make your own choices,
Deserves your wrath.

Anger can be a terrible thing when you start to take it out on the
people around you.
Sometimes anger can be a permanent thing.
Everybody must have anger, and in my opinion, God does curse
at anger.
By Mikey W. (fourth grader)

ANGER

Anger lives where the sun never shines,
Where the flowers don't bloom.
When Anger visits make sure
You don't say, "Thank you."
He's just mean, he's awfully bad, and
He will make you really sad.
Be careful Anger hurts other people's feelings.
Anger just doesn't care.
He sits and wonders why he's mad,
He does not know and does not care.
Anger isn't welcomed anywhere.
By Hannah L. (fourth grader)

SAD

Sad lives in a pool of tears,
Anxiously awaits an apology
That may or may not arrive.
Every day he waits for the mail to come.
Through rain, sleet or snow,
The postman comes and goes.
When he receives his letter
He is full of sunshine, no more tears.
By John John L. (fourth grader)

THE GIBB STREET COMMUNITY GARDEN
(Based upon the book *Seedfolks*, written by Paul Fleishmann)

Not long ago I was dumping ground of unused
Furniture and trash,
Maggots and rats.
As people walked by the horrible stench
Would drive away, never stopping to sit on a bench.

One day a little Vietnamese girl planted lima beans
On the edge of the lot near the fence.
Lima beans have the greatest taste.
They bring a smile to your face.

Leona came to the rescue by filling garbage bags,
So full that the weight made them sag.
When the city workers refused to pick up the trash,
She took the problem to them, quite literally.

Sweet peppers are a favorite of Gonzalos,
Who learned English through watching cartoons.
Tio Juan was a baby who changed into a man
Once he had the opportunity to plant again.

Growing lettuce was like having a new baby.
Virgil's father hovered over the plot, as much as
He could, and thought about money, a lot.

Goldenrod makes a "mean" tea
That helps an old woman continue to see.
Her former doctors die, while she plants
Goldenrod on their graves for free.

Turning into beautiful garden
I have helped to bring the community together.
Now serenity fills the air, and I'm no longer a
Vacant lot, forgotten and bare.
By Ms. Groesch and her fourth-grade class

(This was a poem about the book *Seedfolks*, written by Paul Fleishman.
The poem served as a teaching aid for the mural we had created outside of our classroom. It was a class book read as part of the immigration unit.)

During the book study, the main focuses were characterization and the social studies topic of immigration. To study characters, one needs to examine how they look; how they sound; what they wear; their emotions, desires, and beliefs; where they work; their hobbies; their dark secrets; their past; their future goals, hopes, and plans; and their family, friends and relationships. One of the activities we did with this book was that each child chose a character from the story and wrote a "character recipe" about them. We looked at actual recipes to see what types of measurements are used to make different kinds of food and then asked the children to list at least seven to eight ingredients that they think represent this person. The list provided is only to give you suggestions. You make think of your own descriptors. Ask the children to write down a reason for each choice.

Possible Character Traits:

Strong	Youthful
Weak	Fearful
Old	Youthful
Soul searching	Cheerful
Creative	Shy
Leader	Worrior
Hardworking	Old-fashioned
Diligent	Principled
Religious	Anxious
Dutiful	Community-minded
Embarrassed	Self-serving
Bold	Friendly
Spiteful	Concerned
Giving	Lonely
Helpful	Crowd-pleaser
Helpless	Thoughtful

1. _____

2. _____

3. _____

4. _____

5. _____

7. _____

8. _____

9. _____

I've included a few so that you could see how it is done:

Sam's Spicy Salad
Leona's Lovely Lemonade

Ingredients:
3 cups of sliced sweetness
2 cups of sliced red joy separated
Into rings with a hint of laziness

Ingredients:
2 cups bravery
¼ cups of strength
Into rings with a hint of laziness
½ teaspoon of helpfulness
¾ cup of knowledge

Dressing: ⅓ cup of family ties
⅓ cup of kindness
1 teaspoon of religion
¼ cup of oldness
2 tablespoons of humor
2 tablespoons of sternness
½ teaspoon of helpfulness
¼ teaspoon of anger

You can also ask the students to create a new character for the book and share through a class CD. As an end-of-the-unit activity, you may decide to make a lunch in the classroom where students help to make it from the fruits and vegetables referred to in the book.

Chapter 11

WRITING POETRY ACROSS THE CURRICULUM

HAIKU POEMS

A haiku is a seventeen-syllable Japanese type of poem usually about nature or emotions. These haikus are about the prairie, which is a biome that we had as an ongoing study throughout the year.

Oh, small flower white
Thinks of happiness and joy
On a sea of grass
By Lexy P. (fourth grader)

Blows Indian grass
Across the prairie, it waves.
It can be peaceful.
By Danny D. (fourth grader)

Poetry is used throughout the curriculum: literature, science and social studies. As part of the Immigration unit, the class divided into family groups where each group came from a different country in 1915. The stanzas represent the subtopics they researched: why they left their home, who went with them, the hardships they faced, and their experiences going through Ellis Island.

PRECIOUS NORWAY

Leaving our beloved Norway
Snowy mountains and narrow fiords
Saying farewell to our family and friends
Made us feel scared, anxious, worried and hot.
It felt like it went on forever with this week of horror.
The voyage was sweaty, crowded and hot.
Pirates came twice with swords and guns.
I could finally breathe,
With the wonderful fresh air flowing into my hair.
Freedom was so bright.
When I got there, the first thing I did was eat a pear.
The statue that stood for freedom was bright and big;
Copper color and tall.
I liked it so much
To it I wanted to call.
By Danny D. and Gabrielle L. (fourth graders)

MY JOURNEY

Back in Russia the Jews were treated poorly,
That made my family embark on a journey.
The mountains right by my home,
Were shaped just like slim, tall domes.
My ship the Noordam was dirty and hot.
We slept on an uncomfortable cot.
The food was so bad it made everyone
Act really, really sad.
I didn't like what the doctors did
Because I was just a little kid.
They put you through all these
Tests to see if you were one of the best.

We were so happy to be free
I felt like I could act just like me.
I felt just so joyful
That I started to cry with happiness.
By Emily S. (fourth grader)

SCOTLAND

We left our snow-covered Scotland
To find a better life in America.
We had to leave our home, our family,
And our friends.
The ship smelled musty.
We were too cramped.
We were also very hot
And extremely sweaty.
On Ellis Island, we were inspected,
Given a lot of blood tests, which hurt.
Soon after we were released
To make a better life.
The Statue of Liberty
Looked beautiful as it stood,
Gleaming in the sun.
It represented freedom and liberty.
The tears of joy were overwhelming
As we passed the beautiful statue.
By Will R. (fourth grader)

POEMS WRITTEN AS A RESULT OF THE "LONG ROAD TO FREEDOM" UNIT

This unit is a study of how people were forced from their homes in Africa to the New World and what their lives in America were like during slavery times, Jim Crow, and the civil rights era. This is a three-month unit which encompasses all subject areas, including art, such as painting in the style of the story painter Jacob Lawrence; Romare Bearden, who makes collages; and art from Africa.

Here are some poems from that unit:

Black and White should not fight.
We're all equal and have the same rights.
If we work together we can make a difference forever.
For so long and being right, we are not going to fight.
We can believe in our own religion,
And can make our own decisions.
By Anna W. and Reilly K. (fourth graders)

HUMAN RIGHTS

Black and white, brown and yellow,
Some are as weak as a plate of Jell-O.
But just because they can't fight,
Doesn't mean that you are right.
Don't call them horrible things,
They'll feel like birds without wings.
If you were they, how would you feel
Fed only one meal?
Families getting spread apart,
You must of lost your heart.
Before you do it just think,
Getting kidnapped as fast as a blink.
By Kelly Z. (fourth grader)

HOW THE WIND CAN CHANGE OUR LIVES

Freedom is like the wind when it blows across the fields.
It comes and then it's gone, but you know it will always return.
Freedom changes the way everybody acts, like how the wind
Blows the grass from side to side, making it sway.
The Blacks rejoice now that they can rest.
Whites are upset or rejoice depending upon
How they felt before.
Either way, no one can change the laws now,
Just like no one can stop the wind from blowing the leaves
From the trees or the blades of grass from side to side.
By Rebecca G. (fourth grader)

DIFFERENCES

Differences are everywhere.
People are like snowflakes,
No two beliefs and dreams are the same.
Some are black and some are white,
But that's no reason why you fight.
Joining hands is what should be,
So everyone can have simplicity.
Simple, okay and hard ways,
Everyone's just like the sun's rays.
When one's gone we all fall apart,
But everyone has an equal heart.
By Kelly Z. (fourth grader)

Leave in the winter on a Saturday night when the water is frozen.
When you see the quilt on the house you know there's safety.
When you get past the river you don't have to worry.
Left foot, peg foot will show you the way to safety.
When you get to the Promised Land you know you'll be free.
By Rebecca G. and Brayden M. (fourth graders)

Personification is an important tool for the children to use. The main emphasis is *person*, which relates an object, feeling, or some other noun to a person. The assignment was to think of an emotion as a person and supply them with all the characteristics you would if you were studying a person.

Here is an example of personification:

BLUE

Blue can be loneliness or even sadness.
Blue never comes out, never says anything.
Blue might think of something, but never seems to do much.
His ratty hair frames his red face.
His breath reeks of stinky rotten cheese.
His mean look scares people away.
His mouth reveals his crooked, discolored, chipped teeth
Against his disgustingly rough skin.
The skin on his face is like a bumpy dirt road.
Maybe one day Blue won't be lonely anymore.
By Reilly K. (fourth grader)

Chapter 12

MENTORED BY THE MASTERS

E ach child studied one poet. They needed to learn about the poet's
life, select a favorite poem, explain why they liked it, and write a
poem in the style of that poet. I supplied them with books about their
poets. There is a series of books named *Poetry for Young People,* published
by the Sterling Publishing Company of New York City. A number of authors have written these books.

Here are some examples:

Carl Sandburg
By Michael H. (fourth grader)

Carl Sandburg was born the son of Swedish immigrants, August and
Clara Anderson Sandburg. His family called Carl Charlie. He was the
second of seven children in 1878. He worked from time to time as a
child. He quit school following his eighth grade graduation in 1891. He
spent a decade working in a variety of jobs and then began traveling as
hobo until 1897.

His experiences working and traveling greatly influenced his writing. When the Spanish-American War broke out, Sandburg joined the
service as a voluntary soldier. At the age of seventy he went to Puerto
Rico where he spent his last days battling heat and insects.

Sandburg wrote about the common causes and was called "the voice of the people." He wrote extensively about Illinois. He was a wanderer and always wanted to try new things and go to new places. He married Paula, had hard life experiences, and lost several of children. Sandburg usually wrote in free verse.

My favorite poem is called "Landscape."
See the trees lean to the wind's way of leaning.
See the dirt of the hills shape to the water's
Way of leaning.
See the lift of it all go the way the biggest
Wind and the strongest water want it.

Here is a poem I have written in his style.
The average person is like an ant
Moving all around.
And if you're a student waiting for recess
You're like a tiger ready to pounce.
And if you're like me sitting here with nothing to do,
Then you're bored, you're human.

Emily Dickinson
By Emily W. (fourth grader)

Emily Dickinson was born on December 10, 1830 in Amherst, Massachusetts. The Dickinson family was well known in Amherst, MA. Emily's grandfather was one of the founders of Amherst College, and her father served as a lawyer. He also served in powerful positions in the General Court of Massachusetts, the Massachusetts State Senate and the United States House of Representatives. Emily attended the Amherst Academy. Emily was beautiful, but she was also shy and quiet. When she returned from college she began to wear all white. In her twenties she began writing poetry. When the Civil War began she continued to write, but she became sad. There were changes in her poetry because of the war. The minute her first volume appeared in 1890, Dickenson's poetry was recognized. She wrote over one thousand, seven hundred seventy-five poems during her life. She lived in Amherst until her death from Bright's disease on May 15, 1886.

Emily Dickinson wrote many poems about animals and nature. She would write in stanzas and she also used the first line of her poetry as the title of the poem.

My two favorite poems by the author are "I'm Nobody, Who are You?" and "She Sweeps With Many Colored Brooms." In the poem about the colored brooms Dickinson compares a housewife sweeping to the nature, and the colors it provides.

She sweeps with many colored brooms.
And leaves the shreds behind.
Oh, housewife in the evening west.
Come back, and dust the pond!
You dropped a purple raveling in,
You dropped an amber thread.
And now you've littered all the east
With duds of emerald fly.
And still she flies her spotted brooms,
And still the aprons fly.
Till brooms fade softly into starts—
And then I come away.

I wrote "Nighttime Falls" in the style of Emily Dickinson.

NIGHTTIME FALLS

Nighttime falls.
Here comes the moon.
It is so dark.
It will be morning soon.
Coyotes howl as dogs bark.
Stray cats and dogs run around
In the park.
Moon goes away.
Here comes the sun.
Let's go outside and have some fun.
Frogs in the pond,
Birds in their nests,
Let's lay in the grass
And take a rest.
The sun goes down.
Here comes the moon.
Let's go to bed.
It will be morning soon.
Nighttime Falls.

Gwendolyn Brooks
By Molly H. (fourth grader)

Gwendolyn Brooks was born on June 7, 1917 in Topeka, Kansas. She was the first child of David Brooks and Keziah Brooks. Shortly after her birth they moved to Chicago, which why she is considered to be a Chicagoan. She attended Hyde Park High School, transferred to Black Wendell, and then to the integrated Englewood High School. In 1936 she graduated from Wilson Junior College.

Her profound interest in poetry influenced much of her early work. Her first poem was "Eventide." It was published in *America Childhood Magazine* in 1930. A few years later she met James Weldon Johnson and Langston Hughes, who urged her to read the works of e. e. cummings, T.S. Eliot, and Ezra Pound. She married James in 1938 and her first book was published in 1945.

Gwendolyn Brooks wrote poems about what had happened or what she thought was going to happen. She wrote about the lives of the Negros. Most of her poems are short in length, but are very meaningful.

One of my favorite poems is called "Martin Luther King, Jr."

A man went forth with gifts.
He was a prose poem.
He was a tragic grace.
He was a warm music.
He tried to heal the vivid volcanoes.
The ashes are reading the world.
His dream still wishes to anoint
The barricades of faith
And of control.
His word still burns in the
Center of the sun,
Above the thousands and
The hundreds thousands of years.

The word was justice.
It was spoken.
So it shall be spoken.
So it shall be done.

She wrote about the importance of Martin Luther King. I wrote about Harriet Tubman, another famous African American.

HARRIET TUBMAN

Lead the way
And too proud to say
She brought over three hundred passengers
To freedom,
Nineteen trips to be exact.
And never got owned again.
When she was a soldier she was a little bit older.
She led seven hundred fifty slaves
Through the dark and rainy days
TO FREEDOM.

Jane Yolen
By Charlie D. (fourth grader)

Jane Yolen was born on February 11, 1939 in New York City. Her father was a café journalist, writing columns for a New York paper. Her brother Steven was born a few years later. Jane took piano lessons and studied ballet. She tested and was accepted in to Hunter Junior High School. After a couple of years she was accepted in an art and music school. She attended camp in Vermont during the summer. When she returned she attended Bedford High School where she was very active. She was the captain of the basketball team, the news editor of the school newspaper and the vice president of both the Spanish and Latin clubs. She was a really good student.

As an adult she began writing poems. She has written over two hundred books of poems, songs, and plays. She writes funny poems, rhyming poems. Her audience is children through adults. My favorite poem comes from a book of make-believe animals. She combines two animals into one and then includes characteristics of both animals. My favorite poem is "Mustanks" from her book *Animal Fare*.

THE MUSTANKS

From out of the West since it was won
We've cow and horse herds by the ton.
But Mustank herds? Why, we have none,
Though Mustanks are in town.
They gallop by in thunderous herds
And frighten children, men, and birds;
And for their smell there are no words,
When Mustanks are in town.
So if you see a cloud go by,
And hear a wild, forsaken cry,
Just hold your nose—or you'll know why:
DHU MUSTAGES ARH IN DOWN.

I wrote a poem entitled "The Cattleloaf" in the style of Jane Yolen.

THE CATTLELOAF

The cattleloaf roam around
On the dry, dry desert ground,
Walking into stores in town.
Eating bread, finding food,
They are always in a happy mood.
And if you see one,
You should run, run, run!
Up and down and up and down,
Go cattleloaf on the ground.
Watch out! Cattleloafs are
Coming to town!

Jack Prelutsky
By Elise D. (fourth grader)

Jack Prelutsky was born in Brooklyn, New York on September 8, 1940. He grew up in the Bronx. He lived in a neighborhood made up of Jewish, Irish, and Italian families where everyone knew each other. He grew up in a six-floor apartment building. He attended the high school of Music and Art and for college he went to Hunter. He says in grade school he hated poetry because of the way in which he was taught. He first married a French woman and they got divorced in 1979. He is presently married to Carolyn.

He uses silly words, spaces, rhythms, and he usually throws in some talking animals and make-believe words. All of his poetry is humorous. My favorite poem is "The Early Worm."

An early worm got out of bed
And murmured I feel mean.
I'll put my darkest glasses on
And paint myself bright green.
I'll dress up in my wildest wig,
the one with the purple bangs.
I'll also wear a pair of horns and fangs.
The early worm poked up its head
Which looked a perfect fright.
An early bird observed the worm
And lost his appetite.

I wrote, "There's a Monster" in the style of the poet.

THERE'S A MONSTER

There's a monster in there
With thick long greasy purple hair.
He's harmless in the light of day,
But in the night he's mean I say.
He'll put salt and pepper on your toes
And if you're not careful
He'll bite off your nose.
He drools all over your bed
And you sleep in he'll come
Out of the closet and bite off your head.
I know he's stalking my bed right now.
Before I got in bed tonight
I was having a cow.
I know I'll go in my mom and dad's bed.
Now I can sleep and rest my head.

Ogden Nash
By Mikey W. (fourth grader)

Ogden Nash was born in Rye, New York on August 19, 1902 and died on May 14, 1971. He grew up going to school in New Port, Rhode Island and attended Harvard University. He only attended for one year because of family issues. He decided to get a job and became a teacher. He taught fourteen year olds. Ogden Nash would sit down and visualize something in the past and just start to write. He also loved writing funny poems. He got an award for being America's Humorous Poet. He wrote about feelings and actual events. His favorite poem is everything that happened in his life following a thunderstorm.

My favorite poem is "The Porcupine." It is a poem about a hound and a porcupine. The hound laughs at the porcupine for sitting on a splinter of wood.

I wrote a poem called "Here Comes a Tornado" in the style of Ogden Nash.

HERE COMES A TORNADO

The sky darkens and turns green.
The wind bends the trees as you see.
Suddenly, the sky becomes a fiend.
Whirling, tossing and pushing me.
I hear mother frantically calling me.
Rushing down to the basement
Staying with my family is the key
You can even smell its scent.
My babysitter crying at me.
The dog cowers in the corner.
Mom is comforting sister Bee.
Suddenly, the tornado is over.

Robert Frost
By Ray W. (fourth grader)

Robert Frost was born Mary 26, 1874 in San Francisco where his father was a journalist. His early life was bad because his father died and he had to live with his mean grandfather in New England. He began writing poetry at the age of seventeen. After his first poem was published, he was encouraged to become a poet. His grandfather bought him a farm that he had to work on for ten years and that gave the idea of writing his famous poem, "The Mending Wall."

One of the major influences on his writing came when a book of his poetry was published in England. Sometimes he would carry a book of British poems around with him all day. He would read them over and over again. Robert Frost was a journalist, but he hated to wake up every morning and ask people questions.

Frost loved high school and graduated with top honors. He met the woman he was going to marry in high school. Later he went to Harvard, but dropped out after his son died. It was a sad time when Elliot, his first son, passed away. His later life was a happier time because he had three children in five years following his first son's death. This is the poem I wrote in the style of Robert Frost.

THE TREE

In the autumn the maple tree
Turns gold, burnt orange and crimson.
Young children jump up and down
In the piles of discarded leaves.
In winter children see the
Tree's silhouette etched in white
After a snowstorm. Eagerly they
Build a fort under the tree.
In spring the snow melts.
While everything else turns green.
Nature comes alive with birds chirping,
Bees buzzing and lots of activity.
In summer it is warm, even hot,
As children seek shade under
The maple's broad green leaves.

Chapter 13

CONCLUSION

This book reflects over thirty years of teaching poetry. The topics covered in the book are the world, animals, trees, the five senses, color, figurative language (metaphor, simile, personification), different kinds of poems like haiku, parts of speech, different poets, and integration of poets into each major unit, like immigration and the long road to freedom. As the years pass, teachers get better by trying out new ideas. Each year I would publish a book with the students' self-selected poems. Then we would have a poetry tea to celebrate their writing. Each major unit would have a class book and some kind of sharing with the parents. The positive feedback greatly benefited the children in terms of their self-esteem.

Art can be a catalyst for writing, especially in African American studies—including the artists Romare Beardon, who uses collage, and Jacob Laurence, who uses primary colors and basic shapes in his paintings. Children love the chance to do an art activity that inspires writing. Music is also a good vehicle. The end of the book has a poem about a friend written in the style of William Carlos Williams's "So Much Depends Upon," and the other is a good-bye written by a child I had for both the fourth and fifth grades.

FRIEND

So much depends upon a
Friend.

Someone with you to the
End.

Someone to pick you up when you're
Down.

And turns your frown
Upside down.
By Claire A. (fourth grader)

FIELD DAY ENDS THE YEAR

But now you've learned what you need to know
So it's time to take a deep breath and go.
Teachers are so nice and care about their students.
They make learning fun like math my absolute favorite!
They teach you everything you need to know
Like how to work in groups, write a story,
Or even draw using the computer.
When you have a terrific teacher you really don't want to go.
The year flies by with Camp MacLean, big projects and our science fair.
Rope Wizards, all in a twist and Field Day ends the year.
By Annie S. (fifth grader)

Made in the USA
Charleston, SC
05 January 2016